Ndebele History and Culture

South African People

Author
Nathaniel Perry

Copyright Notice

Copyright © 2017 Global Print Digital
All Rights Reserved

<u>Digital Management Copyright Notice</u>. This Title is not in public domain, it is copyrighted to the original author, and being published by **Global Print Digital**. No other means of reproducing this title is accepted, and none of its content is editable, neither right to commercialize it is accepted, except with the consent of the author or authorized distributor. You must purchase this Title from a vendor who's right is given to sell it, other sources of purchase are not accepted, and accountable for an action against. We are happy that you understood, and being guided by these terms as you proceed. Thank you

First Printing: 2017.

ISBN: 978-1-912483-50-1

Publisher: Global Print Digital.
Arlington Row, Bibury, Cirencester GL7 5ND
Gloucester
United Kingdom.
Website: www.homeworkoffer.com

Table of Content

Introduction 1
Chapter One 4
Ndebele 4
   Language, culture and beliefs 5
   Origins 10
   The cave of Gwasa or the Makapansgat massacre 18
Chapter Two 22
The Ndebele in history 22
   Early History 22
   Origins of the name "Ndebele" 28
   The ZAR war against the Ndzundza Ndebele 33
   Msiza settlement at Hartbeesfontein 39
   The resettlement of the Msiza at ODI 42
   KwaMsiza 48
Chapter Three 52
The influence of apartheid 52
   The Ndebele and the apartheid state 52
Chapter Four 83
Ndebele architecture and settlement patterns 83
   Ndebele architecture and settlement patterns 83
   Dwelling forms 86
Chapter Five 95
The role of gender in Ndebele architecture 95
   Gender roles in Ndebele home-making 95
   Gender spaces in Ndebele homestead planning ... 99
   Gender elements of Ndebele settlement 103
   The role of decoration in Ndebele society 104
   Social and Cultural Life 111
   Division of Labor 112
   Personal adornment 113
   Art and Crafts 116
   Courtship and marriage 122

Chapter Six **124**
  Ndebele Religion and Expressive Culture *124*
    Religious Beliefs 124
    Religious Practitioners. 125
    Ceremonies. 125
    Medicine. 128
    Death and Afterlife. 128

Introduction

Ndebele, also called Transvaal Ndebele, any of several Bantu-speaking African peoples who live primarily in the Limpopo and Mpumalanga provinces in South Africa. The Ndebele are ancient offshoots of the main Nguni-speaking peoples and began migrations to the Transvaal region in the 17th century.

The main group of Transvaal Ndebele traces its ancestry to Musi, or Msi, who, with his followers, diverged from a small group of Nguni people migrating down the southeastern coast of Africa and eventually settled in the Transvaal at the site of modern Pretoria. The descendants of Musi's people were joined in the

18th and 19th centuries by Nguni people fleeing from the wars of Dingiswayo and Shaka in Natal. The Transvaal Ndebele survived the Zulu raids by hiding in the bush. As a result, however, they were geographically divided into separate groups.

Like most Nguni peoples, all the Transvaal Ndebele groups resided in hamlets and relied on animal husbandry and the cultivation of corn (maize), millet, beans, sweet potatoes, and various other crops. Polygyny was permitted, and descent, succession, and inheritance followed the male line.

The Ndebele women continue their tradition of creating elaborate beadwork of all sorts and of painting the walls of their homes (both interior and exterior) with strong, brightly coloured geometric designs. Although the modern Ndebele have retained many of their unique customs, urbanization has affected their traditional culture patterns. Many Ndebele men are now employed in towns or mines, and many others are forced to leave their families for extended periods in search of work

Chapter One
Ndebele

The four major ethnic divisions among Black South Africans are the Nguni, Sotho, Shangaan-Tsonga and Venda. The Nguni represent nearly two thirds of South Africa's Black population and can be divided into four distinct groups; the Northern and Central Nguni (the Zulu-speaking peoples), the Southern Nguni (the Xhosa-speaking peoples), the Swazi people from Swaziland and adjacent areas and the Ndebele people of the Northern Province and Mpumalanga. Archaeological evidence shows that the Bantu-speaking groups that were the ancestors of the Nguni migrated down from East Africa as early as the eleventh century.

Language, culture and beliefs

The isiNdebele language, of which there are variations, is part of the Nguni language group. IsiNdebele is one of the 11 official languages recognized by the South African Constitution, and in 2006 it was determined that just under 600 000 South Africans speak isiNdebele as a home language. Similar to the country's other African languages; isiNdebele is a tonal language, governed by the noun which dominates the sentence.

There are three main groups of Ndebele people:

- ➢ The Southern Transvaal Ndebele (now Gauteng and Mpumalanga)

- ➢ The Northern Transvaal Ndebele (now Limpopo Province) around the towns of Mokopane (Potgietersrus) and Polokwane (Pietersburg).

> The Ndebele people of Zimbabwe, who were called the Matabele by the British.

The two South African Ndebele groups were not only separated geographically, but also differed in their language and cultural practices. The Ndebele of the Northern Province consisted mainly of the BagaLanga and the BagaSeleka groups who were influenced by their Sotho neighbours, and adopted much of their language and culture.

The famous house-painting, beadwork and ornamentation often spoken of as Ndebele are produced mostly by the Ndzundza Ndebele of Mpumalanga and Gauteng (Southern Ndebele). This group speaks a variation of isiNdebele that is considered a 'purer' form of the language, and is closely related to the Zulu language. This version is the only written form of the language.

Strongly patriarchal attitudes and practices are evident

in Ndebele communities. Perhaps more than many other groups, Ndzundza men – especially those of chiefly background – continue to practice polygamy. Women must practice *ukuhlonipha* (respect) towards their husbands and parents-in-law in particular, but also towards men in general. Making and selling beadwork, mats, dolls and other crafts have thus provided some Ndebele women with an independent livelihood. These include internationally famous women like Esther Mahlangu – who has been commissioned to paint her designs on BMWs and South African Airways jets - and those with humbler aspirations.

Rites of passage or initiation ceremonies are practiced among the Ndebele; *Ukuwela* is a male initiation that marks the passage from childhood to adult status. Through the process of initiation, young boys are inducted into traditional lore and the deep mysteries of the group. This knowledge is passed on from one generation of initiates to the next, ensuring that the transfer of knowledge is maintained.

One of the occasions on which isikhethu is enunciated through beaded and decorative clothing is *iqhude* (girl's initiation), which occurs at puberty. At a wedding, female participants also dress in elaborate ceremonial clothing. Here, the bride and her female relatives and attendants are dressed in beaded aprons and necklaces. For both these rituals, the financial provision for a young woman's finery is made by a male relative. These colourful clothes also bear vivid testimony to the distinctiveness of Ndebele culture within the broader world of inter-ethnic politics.

Ndebele people have always managed to retain their cultural practices. More recently, women in Ndzundza society have come to be thought of as the custodians of *isikhethu* (lit. "that which is ours") which consists of the relationships, beliefs and practices on which the very essence of Ndebele identity is centred. Alongside the care of ageing in-laws, and the socialisation of and inculcation of values in children, this role includes the manner in which women clothe their bodies in various ceremonial contexts.

Some Ndebele people converted to Christianity under colonialism and missionary influence. However, although there are many Christian converts, ancestral beliefs have not disappeared. Instead, there has been a mixture of traditional beliefs and Christianity. Ancestral spirits are important in Ndebele religious life, and offerings and sacrifices are made to the ancestors for protection, good health, and happiness.

Ancestral spirits come back to the world in the form of dreams, illnesses, and sometimes snakes. The Ndebele also believe in the use of magic. Ill fortune such as bad luck and illness is considered to be sent by an angry spirit. When this happens, the help of a traditional healer is sought, and he or she will communicate with the ancestors, or use natural herbs and prayers to get rid of the problem.

Origins

Most Ndebele trace their ancestry to the area that is now called KwaZulu-Natal. The history of the Ndebele people can be traced back to Mafana, their first identifiable chief. Mafana's son and successor, Mhlanga, had a son named Musi who, in the early 1600's, decided to move away from his family (later to become the mighty Zulu nation) and to settle in the hills of Gauteng near Pretoria.

After Chief Musi's death, his eldest son, Manala was named future chief. This was challenged by another senior son, Ndzundza and the group was divided by the resulting squabble between the two. Ndundza was defeated and put to flight. He and his followers headed eastwards, settling in the upper part of the Steelport River basin at a place called KwaSimkhulu, near present-day Belfast, leaving Manala to be made chief of his father's domain. Two further factions, led by other sons, then broke away from the Ndebele core. The Kekana moved northwards and settled in the region of present-day Zebediela, and the other section, under Dlomo, returned to the east coast from where the Ndebele had originally come.

By the middle of the 19th century, the Kekana had further divided into smaller splinter groups, which spread out across the hills, valleys and plains surrounding present-day Mokopane (Potgietersrus), Zebediela and Polokwane (Pietersburg). These groups were progressively absorbed into the numerically superior and more dominant surrounding Sotho groups, undergoing considerable cultural and social change. By contrast, the descendants of Manala and Ndzundza maintained a more recognisably distinctive cultural identity, and retained a language which was closer to the Nguni spoken by their coastal forebears (and to present-day isiZulu). Hence, the formation of the Southern vs. Northern Ndebele.

A third group, subjects of the Zulu leader Mzilikazi, fled north from Natal after his defeat by Shaka in 1817. Details of their incorporation into the South African Ndebele groups are confusing and under-researched, but it appears that Mzilikazi settled with a Ndebele group for a period before being defeated by the Voortrekkers in 1836. At this point he trekked over the Limpopo River to present day Zimbabwe, and settled in an area between the Limpopo and the Zambezi Rivers that later became known as Matabeleland. He is therefore credited as being the founder of the Ndebele in Zimbabwe.

By the 1820s, Nzundza homesteads were widely dispersed along the Steelport River. This scatter of homesteads was due in part to raids by Mzilikazi and his followers (mentioned above), but also to factional conflict after the death of Chief Magodongo. From the 1840s, white farmers (Boers), who had been migrating to the Highveld in growing numbers since the 1830s, encroached on the areas occupied by the Ndzundza Ndebele. Boer settlements, established between the Olifants and Steelport rivers, were threatened by the proximity of the chiefly stronghold of Konomtjharhelo, established by the Ndzundza Chief Mabhoko I.

In 1883, during the reign of the Mabhoko, war broke out between the Ndzundza and the (Boer) Zuid-Afrikaansche Republiek (South African Republic). For eight months, the Ndebele held out against the onslaught by hiding in subterranean tunnels in their mountain stronghold at Konomtjharhelo near the town of Roossenekal. From time to time, Mabhoko's brave warriors crept past the enemy lines undetected to fetch water and food. However, after two women of the tribe were ambushed in the nearby woods and tortured, one revealed the Mabhoko's whereabouts. After the Mabhoko's defeat, the cohesive tribal structure was broken up, and the tribal lands confiscated. Despite the disintegration of the tribe, the Ndebele retained their cultural unity.

After 1877, with the British annexation of the Transvaal and the 1879 defeat of the Pedi by the British, the balance of power shifted away from African independent kingdoms in the region. In the autumn of 1883, war broke out between the Boers and the Ndzundza under Nyabela. A strategy of siege and attrition was staged by the Boers under Commandant Pier Joubert.

For eight months, Nyabela, with those Ndzundza who had left their dispersed settlements along the Steelport to group around him, were besieged at Konomtjharhelo. A Boer myth has it that they were hidden in a centralized fortress of interlocking caverns, but recent evidence suggests that the well-armed Ndzundza were dug into a series of fortified settlements which spread over a much wider area. The destruction of Ndebele crops and the seizing of their cattle were largely the undoing of the chiefdom, whose people were gradually starved into submission.

In July Nyabela surrendered and left his capital for the last time, as the victorious Boers torched it behind him. The conditions imposed by the victors onto the vanquished were very harsh. Nyabela and other members of the chiefly family were imprisoned, Ndzundza lands were confiscated and given to the Boers who had participated in the siege, and members of the polity were given to Boers as indentured farm labourers and servants. Nduzundza were thus scattered widely over the southern regions of the Transvaal Republic, including the districts of

Lydenburg, Middeburg, Standerton and Wakkerstroom.

Later, under apartheid, many Ndebele living in the northern Transvaal were assigned to the predominantly seSotho-speaking homeland of Lebowa, which consisted of several segments of land scattered across the northern Transvaal.

Others, mostly southern Ndebele, who had retained more traditional elements of their culture and language, were assigned to KwaNdebele. KwaNdebele had been carved out of land that had been given to the son of Nyabela, a well-known Ndebele fighter in Kruger's time. The homeland was, therefore, prized by Ndebele traditionalists, who pressed for KwaNdebele independence through the 1980s.

KwaNdebele was declared a "self-governing" territory in 1981. However, very few of its 300,000 residents could find jobs in the homeland, so many inhabitants worked in the industrial region of Pretoria and Johannesburg. At least 500,000 Ndebele people lived in urban centres throughout South Africa and in homelands other than KwaNdebele through the 1980s. During the 1980s and the early 1990s, many Ndebele recognized a royal family, the Mahlangu family, and the capital of KwaNdebele was called KwaMhlanga.

The royal family was divided, however, over economic issues and the question of "independence" for the homeland.

These disputes were overridden by the dissolution of the homelands in 1994. At that time, in addition to the estimated 800,000 Ndebele people in South Africa, nearly 1.7 million Ndebele lived in Zimbabwe (Matabele), where they constituted about one-sixth of the population, and another 300,000 lived in Botswana.

The cave of Gwasa or the Makapansgat massacre

In September 1854, 28 Boers were killed in what would later become the Northern Transvaal. These Boers were killed in three separate incidents by an alliance of the Ndebele chiefdoms of Mokopane and Mankopane. In anticipation of a military retaliation that he knew would come, Mokopane and his followers retreated into some caves. In late October two Boer commandos and their Kgatla allies attacked the caves, but failed to take them or force the people out. The commandos laid siege to the caves.

The siege lasted about three weeks. By the end of the siege, between 1 000 and 3 000 people in the caves had died, and many others had been captured as prisoners of war and enslaved. In addition, the Boers took 6 300 cattle, 1 200 goats and 450 kg of ivory. On the Boer side, there were few deaths from the siege. A major casualty, however, was Piet Potgieter. He was shot from inside the cave. The number of deaths among the Kgatla allies are unknown. This event has come to play a central role in the development of Afrikaner nationalism. From the Boer perspective, African "savages," without any reason, had killed the Boers when all they were trying to do was to extend "civilisation." Indeed, the "murders" of Boers in this version are referred to as a "massacre."

The death of Mokopane and his many followers, however, was not considered to be important enough to be called a massacre. But there were reasons the Ndebele attacked the Boers in the 1850s. The people of Mokopane and Mankopane had been subjected to raids for cattle and people to enslave. We have an account of how these raids worked. Here is a report of how Hermanus Potgieter, well known as a raider, operated:

"They spanned out their wagons at the foot of a rise on which there stood a native village. Presently a couple of natives came down the hill to the encampment and greeted Potgieter. Upon this, he drew out a ramrod and stuck it upright in a neighbouring ant heap and pointed to it, but said nothing. The two natives returned to the village and came back presently bringing a couple of slaughter goats. H. Potgieter said never a word but looked sternly at them and pointed to the ramrod. They went back and fetched an ox. H. Potgieter still pointed to the ramrod. Then they went and fetched a couple of tusks of ivory and put them down, but the ramrod remained erect"¦. Hermanus Potgieter and his men mount[ed] their horses, r[o]de around the hill and up to the kraal and [shot] some natives. Presently they came back driving the cattle to the camp and a number of captured children "¦ that was the requirement when the ramrod was stuck upright."

It was against such raids and encroachment on their lands and resources by the Boers that the incident had occurred.

According to most accounts, including oral traditions, these attacks had been intended to chase the Boers away from Ndebele lands.

Nathaniel Perry

Chapter Two
The Ndebele in history
Early History

Few Southern African indigenous groups have so captured the interest of the world as have the South amaNdebele of the central highveld, an area previously known as the Transvaal but today incorporated into the Gauteng and Northern Provinces. Their highly colourful and intricately painted homesteads, their skilled and varied beadwork, their clear language of architecture, and their stately forms of dress have made them a popular field of research with artists, architects and social anthropologists. They have also become a major focus of interest for many visitors to this country.

It is generally accepted today that the South Ndebele migrated onto the central highveld of southern Africa some four centuries ago. The exact date of their arrival is difficult to determine, but estimates tend to vary from 1485 by Fourie, through to the 1630-1670 period established by Van Warmelo. The latter dating is today regarded as the more reliable of the two.

Both Fourie and Van Warmelo are in agreement that, despite the fact that the Ndebele settled in a predominantly Sotho-Tswana speaking area, they have retained their customs and Nguni language roots with "remarkable tenacity". However some researchers have suggested a Sotho influence in some rituals and aspects of material culture, and more recent research into their architecture, settlement patterns, and methods of construction seem to indicate a definite

Pedi-Tswana influence, even allowing for the adaptations one has come to expect of a culture moving from the grass-rich coastal lands east of the Drakensberge to the more extreme thermal variations found on the South African Highveld.

Details regarding the Ndebele prior to their arrival on the highveld are scarce, and their recorded history only begins with the names of their first two kings, Mafana and Mhlanga. Following Mhlanga's death the clan became embroiled in a protracted struggle which eventually brought his son, Musi, to the leadership. By that stage the group had already moved to Mnyamana, near Wonderboompoort, immediately north of the future Boer town of Pretoria. Musi, in his turn, had five sons: Manala, Masombuka, Ndzundza, Mathombeni and Dhlomu. Upon his death Musi was buried beneath a tree at Wonderboompoort, a location which is still visited by his descendants to the present day. Almost inevitably his sons quarreled over their inheritance and, as a result, the clan split into a number of smaller groups, the largest two coalescing under the leaderships of Manala and Ndzundza respectively. Masombuka left briefly but rejoined Manala later on, while Dhlomu and some of his followers are reputed to have returned to KwaZulu. For the purpose of subsequent Ndebele history the Manala were held to be the senior of the two groups.

In due course Ndzundza was succeeded by his son Mxetsha who, in his turn, was succeeded by his son Magoboli. Magoboli was followed by his son Bongwe, who unfortunately only reigned for three years, and as a result of his premature death, his brother Sindeni was appointed as regent. At this time, for reasons that are not known, there was a shift in the line of succession, which allowed Sindeni's son, Mahlangu, to follow his father. As a result the ruling family, which had previously been known as the Mdungwa, now became the Mahlangu. The last of these events probably took place in the latter part of the mid-eighteenth century.

Mahlangu was succeeded by his son Phaswana, who was followed in his turn by Maridili, who was followed in rapid order by his four sons, Mdalanyana, Mgwezana, Dzele and Mxabule. The last, Mxabule, was murdered by his nephew Magodongo, the son of his older brother Mgwezana, who then became head of the Ndzundza. In 1823 the amaKumalo under Mzilikazi invaded the highveld, and in about 1825 they attacked the Ndzundza, burning their capital at Mnyamana, and killing Magodongo together with all his sons from his Right-hand House. The remnants of the Ndzundza fled from Mnyamana under the leadership of Mabhogo, a younger son of Magodongo and the only survivor of his Left-hand House, and settled at Namashaxelo, near the site of the latter-day Boer village of Roossenekal. At this time Mabhogo, who ruled until 1865, entered into an alliance with the neighbouring Pedi chief Malewa, and it seems probable that the alterations in Ndebele material culture can be dated from this time onwards.

In 1847 Mabhogo was visited for the first time by groups of disaffected Dutch farmers from the Cape, better known as Voortrekkers, who rapidly came to know the Ndebele as either the Mapog, Mapogga, Mapoers, Mapoch or M'pogga. Although most Ndebele today find this form of address derogatory, many South Africans sadly still persist with this form of address.

Almost from the onset sporadic skirmishes began to take place between these new immigrants, or Boers as they became known, and the Ndebele-Pedi alliance, who actively resisted the incursions which they were beginning to make upon their ancestral lands. In 1864 the alliance was attacked, and defeated, by a Swazi force acting at the instigation of the Boers, leaving the Dutch in the rear-guard to conduct a simple mopping-up operation of survivors. Soon thereafter, in 1865,

Mabhogo died, leaving the Ndebele to sort out a complex and bitter inheritance struggle. As a result Ndebele leadership passed to the Masilela family. Soqaleni ruled until 1873, followed by Xobongo, a tyrant who ruled until 1879, when he was succeeded by Nyabele.

Origins of the name "Ndebele"

The name, Ndebele, was probably derived from the Sotho-Tswana term "tebele", meaning a stranger, or one who plunders. They share in this appellation with at least three other South African groups, the most famous being the amaKumalo, an Nguni-speaking group who, under the leadership of Mzilikazi, migrated from northern KwaZulu in 1823, and after a residence of some thirteen years on the highveld, moved to western Zimbabwe in 1837, where they became know by the Shona variant of Matabele. The name has also been applied to the North Ndebele, originally a Venda-speaking group who settled in the Pietersburg area and became acculturised by their Sotho-speaking neighbours; and the baTlokwa, a Sotho-speaking group who joined the British invasion of KwaZulu in 1879, and in consequence were awarded land in the Nqutu region of KwaZulu-Natal. The term is therefore consistent with the idea of being a stranger, an invader, or perhaps even a refugee into a region.

A brief history of polygamy in Southern Africa

One of the preconceptions more popularly held by both academics and lay public alike in regard to southern African rural society is that the indigenous family unit is polygamous in nature. This is only partly true. A broad survey of homestead patterns in the region reveals that whilst a number of polygamous settlements may still be found in the rural countryside, these are in a distinct minority, and monogamous marriages appear to be the general norm. It could of course be argued that this is a recent development brought about by the work of Christian missionaries, but the validity of such an assumption needs be questioned. Not only do the Christian churches which enjoy the largest following in southern Africa, the so-called Independent Churches, permit their followers to practice polygamy, but although the practice of polygamy was indeed more prevalent during the last century, its presence was not as widespread as various missionaries way have wished us to believe. Lichtenstein wrote of the Xhosa in 1812 that:

"Most of the Koossas have but one wife; the kings and chiefs of the kraals only have four or five."

This was reinforced by Alberti who stated, also of the Xhosa, that:

"Those with least resources, must be satisfied with one woman, others have two, and rarely more."

Contemporary visitors to other parts of the country have come to similar conclusions. Livingstone went one step further and in 1857 estimated that approximately 43% of Tswana men practiced polygamy, and then only a very small minority of these had more than three wives. By 1946 an official census revealed that this figure had dropped to 11% with only 1.3% having three wives or more.

The practice of polygamy may, in most cases, be explained in terms of a levirate, a social practice, used to ensure the continued status and survival of widows and orphans within an established family structure. While it is true, therefore, that every rural family is potentially polygamous in nature, we need to question whether such polygamy was the result of "male sexuality and lust", as the missionaries would have it, or merely the enforcement of social obligations intended to reinforce ties between family or clan groupings. Recent data would seem to show that some

27% of rural households are currently headed by widowed or single women. If we were to assume that in the 1850s an equivalent number of women could have become widows and were thus absorbed into the monogamous households of family members, thus making them polygamous, then it will be seen that this form of union could have accounted for most of the polygamous marriages recorded by Livingstone among the Tswana. The remaining group, those with three wives or more, were a distinct minority and their polygamy may be explained in terms of group leaders creating political alliances and gaining control of resources for their own communities.

The general trend away from polygamous unions evidenced since 1900 could therefore be explained in two ways. The growth of urbanisation and the establishment of urban-based political structures has brought about a decreased emphasis upon both regional group identity and the power of the traditional and inherited rural leadership. The need for making unions based upon political expediency has thus lessened considerably. The economics of obtaining a bride in the rural areas has also changed substantially over the past five generations, as women also began to enter the ranks of an industrialised and urban proletariat in increasing numbers after the 1930s.

The conclusion therefore is that the practice of polygamy may have been common in southern Africa up to the end of the last century but that it was never as widespread as has been popularly represented.

The ZAR war against the Ndzundza Ndebele

The leadership of Nyabele was to mark the final era of Ndzundza Ndebele independence. On 13 August 1882 the Pedi paramount chief Sekhukhune was killed, together with fourteen of his advisors. The assassins were acting at the behest of Mampuru, Sehukhune's half brother, who had previously contested the Pedi chieftainship in 1861, and who, under the British administration of the Transvaal, had acted as chief during Sekhukhune's imprisonment in Pretoria from 1879 to 1881.

The ZAR Government, conscious of its newly-won independence from the British, was determine to exercise its authority over the Pedi and demanded that Mampuru be handed over for trial. Mampuru then fled and sought refuge with the Ndzundza, who had previously supported him in 1861 in his claim for the Pedi leadership. The Volksraad of the ZAR demanded his apprehension, but Nyabele not only declined to hand over Mampuru, but also refused to pay the customary Hut Tax to the new Transvaal government. Although largely symbolic, this gesture was also an open act of defiance which proclaimed Ndzundza independence from the ZAR and refuted Boer claims of suzerainty over his people.

Given their precarious hold over their indigenous subjects, this was not a challenge which the newly established ZAR could afford to ignore, Consequently on 30 October 1882 a burgher commando under the leadership of Gen Piet Joubert set out from Middelburg and invested the Ndzundza mountain stronghold near Namashaxelo. In reality this was little more than a series of caves where Nyabele and his people had thought of making a tactical retreat. No records exist of the exact number of Boers engaged in this campaign but, judging from General Joubert's letters, it appears that no more than 1000 to 2000 men were ever in the field at any one time.

Certainly the Boers do not appear to have had much stomach for the fight, leading Joubert to complain to the Volksraad that the burghers "seemed to prefer looting cattle for their own account". After a long campaign of nearly nine months, the Ndzundza, starved and dynamited into submission, capitulated and handed Mampuru, bound hand and foot, over to the Boers. Both Mampuru and Nyabele were taken prisoner to Pretoria where they were tried for insurrection and sentenced to death. The British, who had previously supported Mampuru's claims to the Pedi leadership, attempted to intercede on their behalf with the ZAR, but their efforts were only partially successful, for while Nyabele's sentence was commuted to life imprisonment, Mampuru was hanged in Pretoria Prison on 22 November 1883.

At the same time the Volksraad declared the Ndzundza ancestral lands to be forfeit to the ZAR Government, which then proceeded to parcel them out to members of Joubert's commando. The surviving Ndzundza were indentured for five years as labourers to the farmers in the district, thus effectively scattering them and breaking their power as a tribe forever.

In retrospect the ZAR Government might appear to have acted in a somewhat precipitous manner in what was, after all, an internecine squabble which did not present them with an immediate threat. However, for the ZAR the question of Pedi succession was a sensitive one which needs to be read in conjunction with political conditions prevailing in the Transvaal at the time. Since the establishment of the Transvaal Republic in 1852, the region had remained in an almost constant state of anarchy.

The wars against the Tswana in 1852 and 1858, and against Makapane in 1854; the rise of separate Boer republics at Utrecht (1854), Lydenburg (1856), and Zoutpansberg (1857); the establishment of a Boer revolutionary government in the Waterberg in 1860 and the four years of civil war which followed it; the

Swazi attack upon the Ndebele, instigated by the Boers in 1864; the war against the Venda, the Boer retreat from the Zoutpansberg and the destruction of Schoemansdal by the Venda in 1867; and the disastrous war upon the Pedi in 1877, all depleted its resources, and by the time the British annexed the Transvaal on 12 April 1877 its government was bankrupt and on the point of collapse.

Boer independence from British rule was only regained after a brief series of battles in 1881, and thus it was to be expected that any challenge made against the newly-established government of the ZAR would be met with harsh and immediate force. The newly-elected Volksraad must have been understandably anxious to avoid a return to conditions prevailing in the Transvaal five years previously while, at the same time, serving notice to British and Black alike that it was determined to maintain the independence it had regained only the previous year.

Msiza settlement at Hartbeesfontein

During the years of Nyabele's imprisonment, some of his family and personal advisers were allowed to settle on the white-owned farm of Hartbeesfontein, located between Wonderboom and Derdepoort north of Pretoria, in order to be near him. These were lands previously occupied by the Ndebele prior to their move to Namashaxelo, but which had since been annexed by the Transvaal government for white occupation. Shortly before the outbreak of the South African War of 1899-1902 Nyabele was granted a pardon. However he was not allowed to return to Namashaxelo but rejoined his followers at Hartbeesfontein where he is believed to have died in about 1903.

He was succeeded by Mfene, the second son of his eldest brother Soqaleni, who had preceded Nyabele as chief of the Ndzundza. Mfene is reported to have lived at Hartbeestfontein for a few years before moving with the bulk of his family and followers to a site on the upper reaches of the Wilge River, known as Weltevrede, near Vaalfontein. Mfene was followed by his son Maysha and, when he died in about 1951, he was succeeded by Mabusa David Mahlangu who continues to reside at Weltevrede.

The contingent of Nyabele's immediate family and followers included Kgalabi (also given as Umghalabi) Msiza whose family, the Msiza, traditionally enjoyed the high status of "shield-bearers to the Ndzundza king". He settled at Hartbeesfontein where, in time, he became the patriarch of a substantial extended family. His first wife, Usmeshe, raised a family which included six sons, while his second, Nomatombeni Dina Mahlangu, bore him another five. The number of daughters in the family is not known. Nomatombeni was the daughter of Nyabele and his wife Sibiya, and probably met and married Kgalabi at Hartbeesfontein.

When Mfene and the majority of his retinue relocated to Weltevrede, for reasons which are not clear the Msiza family chose to remain at Hartbeesfontein where they continued to farm their lands. By all accounts they flourished, and by the 1950s Kgalabi's extended family settlement included the homesteads of nine sons, three of whom had two wives each. The settlement also included the home of Zondiwe Jacob Bhuda, who had married Umdundwana Amy Msiza, daughter of Kgalabi's brother, who probably joined the Hartbeesfontein community after Mfene's group had departed for Weltevrede.

The date of Kgalabi's death is not known, but can probably be assumed to have taken place during the 1930s or the early 1940s Leadership of the Hartbeesfontein community thereafter devolved upon Hlangane Speelman Msiza, his oldest son by his senior wife, Usmeshe. In time Hlangane became known to his white neighbours as Cornelius Speelman.

The resettlement of the Msiza at ODI

Despite the fact that the Msiza family continued to live and farm at Hartbeesfontein, the property remained in the ownership of a family called Wolmarans. At that time it was a common arrangement for black farmers living on "white" land to exchange their labour for a small piece of ground where they could build their homesteads and plant a small crop. However, they had no title to this land, no tenure or work contracts, and could lose their homes at the whim of the white owner. By all accounts Wolmarans was considered to have been "a good man", and the Msiza remained at Hartbeesfontein for nearly sixty years. When Wolmarans died in about 1952, his son-in-law found it expedient to sell the property to the developers of the new Wonderboom airport, and the Msiza were forced to find new homes elsewhere.

By this time the Ndebele had begun to decorate the walls of their homesteads with a variety of polychromatic designs, and at an early stage the practice had come to the notice of architects, artists and anthropologists. Among them was Prof AL Meiring, Head of the School of Architecture at Pretoria University. He appears to have begun visiting the Msiza at Hartbeesfontein early in the 1950s, and at one stage he and his students drew up a detailed record of the settlement. When the family found itself in the position of being evicted from their homes, Meiring interceded on their behalf with the authorities and made it possible for them to be resettled in an area known as Klipgat, in the district of Odi, located some 50km north of Pretoria. Meiring further facilitated the move by obtaining grants of building materials for the family, most particularly timber and thatch.

By 1953 the Msiza, under the leadership of Hlangane, had rebuilt their homes at Odi and their old homestead at Hartbeesfontein had been demolished. They were joined in the move by members of the Bhuda and Skosana families, who had married Msiza women and now belonged to the extended Msiza family group. One additional family, also called Msiza but not directly related to the Kgalabi line, also made its home at Odi. Initially this move involved some 21 nuclear families, but as at least three of the men were polygamous, the number of families units was probably closer to eighteen.

In the 1960s Hlangane Msiza died, and leadership of what had by now grown into a village passed on to his brothers. Today this rests with Hlangane's last surviving brother, Maselwane Msiza who, despite his advanced age, still enjoys good health and clear thinking. His memories of events at Hartbeesfontein, and thereafter, form the basis for much of what has been related here.

Although never given an official name, the village began to appear on road signs and various large-scale maps as either KwaMapoch, Speelman's Kraal, or simply as The Ndebele Village. Its residents however, prefer the term KwaMsiza, which translates to "the place of the Msiza".

By the 1960s the village had become a popular stopping point for tourists, a factor assisted by the South African Tourist Board who placed it upon its itineraries of local attractions, and its residents had begun to supplement their income through the manufacture and sale of beaded artifacts. It did not take long for Msiza women to develop a name for themselves as excellent bead workers, and their handiwork was to inspire similar developments among other Ndebele families in the region. Articles about the Msiza and their colourful, polychromatic habitat began to be carried by numerous journals, both local and overseas, thus increasing their fame as a community of artists.

Unfortunately, the agricultural lands allocated to the Msiza were neither suitable for planting, nor were they large enough to sustain the growing community. As a result many of its menfolk, as well as some of the women, were forced to enter the migrant labour market. In most cases this took them away from home for eleven months of the year, and although their income helped to sustain their families, their absence from home for such long periods had a negative effect upon the quality of life now enjoyed in the village. Most of the responsibility for the raising of children now fell upon the women, and although this was not unique to the Msiza in the context of the Apartheid society which developed in South Africa during the 1950s and 1960s, the Ndebele reaction to this oppression had some unique and interesting results.

This was most marked in such areas as wall decoration and codes of ceremonial female dress.

During the 1960s and early 1970s the people of KwaMsiza were to enjoy a period of relative stability and prosperity. Assisted by grants of thatching grass and paint from the South African Tourist Board, they continued to maintain their homes to a standard which continued to attract visitors to their homes and clients for their beadwork. Work was also available, and although absent from their families as migrant workers, the men were able to earn money on a constant basis. However, by the mid-1970s the nation-wide drought had begun to have a serious effect upon the already meager crops they could grow. Their economic well-being was aggravated after June 1976 when a national student revolt made international headlines and heralded the beginning of a more intensive resistance against white Apartheid government. Although the district was not directly involved in the events of 1976, many whites were deterred from entering black residential areas by both the threat of violence as well as the ominous presence of South African security forces, and the number of visitors to the village dropped dramatically. Added to this was the fact that many men, previously employed in the migrant labour market, lost their jobs and returned home to their families, thus increasing their financial burden.

KwaMsiza

KwaMsiza is a village of 49 families located some 50km north of Pretoria. Its residents are Ndzundza Ndebele, and belong to three major family groups: the Msiza, the Bhuda, and the Skosana. They originally lived on the farm Hartbeesfontein, at Wonderboompoort, but when this land was expropriated to make way for an airport in 1953, they were relocated to the District of Odi, where they reside to the present day. The village exhibits a number of interesting features, including a number of dwellings built in the historical verandah style, probably derived from the baPedi, as well as a great number of walls painted in a polychromatic manner. The village is also well-known for the excellent beadwork artifacts made by its women.

The history of KwaMsiza has its roots in the ZAR-Ndzundza War of 1882, when a commando of some 2000 Boers attacked the Ndebele capital of Namashaxelo. As a result of this war, the Ndzundza were dispossessed of their ancestral lands in the Middelburg-Grobblersdal district, and their king, Nyabele, was eventually banished to the farm Hartbeesfontein, just north of Pretoria. There he was joined by members of his family, as well as a retinue of followers, among whom were numbered the Msiza, a family who traditionally held the position of "shield-bearers to the king".

After Nyabele's death in 1903, his family moved away, leaving behind one of their daughters, Nomatombeni Dina Mahlangu who had in the meantime married Kgalabi Msiza. The family remained at Hartbeesfontein until 1953, when they were forced to move to KwaMsiza. Although the origins of Ndebele wall decoration are still uncertain, there is good reason to believe that the practice may have been started by the Msiza when they were still living at Hartbeespoort. Today the practice has become widespread, and the use of Ndebele-style decoration has become a matter of national pride, influencing such diverse areas of design as women's fashions, stamps, advertising, and the livery of our national airlines.

Unfortunately the history of the Msiza at Odi has been one of conflict and hardship. Over the years its residents have had to deal not only with the oppression of the Apartheid government in Pretoria and that of its surrogate in Bophuhatswana, but also with constant economic hardship, and the breakdown of many of their traditional social values. Today the family is finally emerging from the hardships of the last 140 years, and through its own industry and creativity, is beginning to play an important role in the affairs of their region.

Chapter Three
The influence of apartheid
The Ndebele and the apartheid state
When the Nationalist Party was elected to power in 1948 by a minority of the white electorate, their platform promised their followers that the white race would continue to dominate all aspects of South African society. Its ideology of "baaskap", or "white power", propounded that all black South Africans belonged to a perpetual rural proletariat, which could be trained to draw water, hew wood, and serve the wishes of its white masters, but which must ever be denied access to higher levels of education. They also

held that the imposition of white rule was necessary to prevent the outbreak of "a racial holocaust", where competing tribal interests would inevitably precipitate the country into a state of violence and anarchy.

Although the nature of Nationalist policy did not change radically for the next twenty years, by the 1960s its dialectic had begun to move from its crude foundations of "white power", to a more systematized usufruct of South Africa's black population as a source of cheap labour. At the same time the Nationalist Government had begun to flesh out Apartheid into a policy of "separate-but-equal" development, which drew heavily upon the works of African-American writers who had begun to publish similar theories during the 1920s.

Ultimately, it claimed, every black South African, whether living in an urban or a rural area, would be allocated to any one of nine self-governing homelands whose citizenship would be based upon the tribal, or ethnic, identity of its members. The anomalies presented by a growing black urban middle class who had found legal residence in the urban areas, and who had become increasingly distanced from its historical roots, were blithely ignored.

It is difficult to establish the exact period when the Ndebele began to develop the concept of a separate cultural polity. Their homesteads only began to be painted by their women in a distinctive polychromatic style sometime between 1937 and 1951, probably soon after the election to power of the Nationalist government in 1948. However, given their status as "Ndebele" immigrants in a highveld region inhabited predominantly by Sotho-Tswana, it is probable that the roots for this consciousness were always present and only became overtly manifest after the rise of white Afrikaner nationalism in South Africa.

Initially the establishment of an Ndebele homeland did not feature high on the Government agenda. By the early 1960s it had identified nine separate "ethnic" groups and the Ndebele were specifically excluded from these designs. Its own ethnographers believed that the groups were too scattered and numerically too few to warrant their own separate homeland. Also, they held that they had become too integrated with their Sotho and Tswana neighbours to be separated at that late stage.

It was true that the Ndebele were indeed scattered over a wide area, consisting of rural clans, labourers residing on white farms, migrating groups and urban elites, and that the two major groupings, the North and the South Ndebele, claimed separate historical roots despite widespread intermarriage. However both groups had managed to develop strong cultural identities separate from their Sotho/Tswana neighbours, which, during the 1950s were manifesting themselves in numerous tribal associations which served as a channel for migrant workers in the affairs of their rural groups and maintained links with their larger clan polities.

Thus although the membership of individual groups was relatively small, cumulatively they constituted a large enough group to warrant recognition by Apartheid's planners, and as early as the 1950s they had begun to protest classification as either Tswana or Pedi.

The reality of the situation was that the ethnic cleansing necessitated by the implementation of a "bantustan" policy had already reached a scale and a level of rural hardship such as to warrant exposure by local researchers and unfavourable coverage by the international media. The removal of a widely scattered group such as the Ndebele presented Apartheid's planners with a problem which even they hesitated to implement.

Nonetheless the granting of "self-government" to Bophuthatswana and Lebowa did little to lessen the idea among many Ndebele that they too warranted a separate homeland. Although these demands were received with a certain amount of glee on the part of Apartheid bureaucrats, who saw this as justification of their ideological planning, the reality of these demands was far removed from Apartheid ideology. Much of it lay in the fact that both Bophuthatswana and Lebowa were refusing to implement separate education for their Ndebele citizens, to recognise siNdebele language, and to issue business permits, ID papers, passports, pension benefits and government jobs to Ndebele citizens who refused to forego their Ndebele identity and adopt Bophuthatswana or Lebowa citizenship.

The first known organisation which actively promoted a Ndebele identity was the Mandebele Cradle Association, founded in about 1957. They were followed in 1965 by the Ndebele Ethnic Group based in Mamelodi and Atteridgeville, and by the Ndebele National Organisation, based in Soweto. On 5 October 1967 members of various Ndebele political and cultural organisations met in Mamelodi and founded the Transvaal NNO. This was a coalition of both North and South Ndebele representing groups from both urban and rural areas. At their conference held in Mamelodi from 31 August to 1 September 1968, the call was first made for the formation of a Ndebele homeland.

Although at this stage a number of rural Ndebele Chiefs had become prominent within the TNNO, the impetus behind the organisation lay with migrant workers on the Witwaterstrand. These included a number of traders, teachers and intellectuals who perceived that their middle class aspirations would be best met by Nationalist Government's policies of "separate development."

Calls for a separate Ndebele homeland were given additional impetus in 1968, after the establishment of a Ndzundza Tribal Authority in the Weltevreden district of Lebowa. Prominent in the movement were SS Skosana, who was later to become Chief Minister of KwaNdebele, Chief David Maisha Mabhogo, Paramount of the Ndzundza, Chief Mabena of the Manala, and Chief Johannes Shikoane Kekana of the North Ndebele. Together they consolidated their grass-root support for a separate Ndebele "Bantustan".

Although their efforts at first proved fruitless, by 1972 the Nationalist government had begun to look upon their demands more favourably. In March 1972 a group of Ndebele leaders and officials from the Department of Bantu Administration and Development met to discuss the issue of a separate Ndebele Homeland; by

September these reached draft stage, and these were finalised in 1973. By this time four South Ndebele tribal authorities had been established: the Ndzundza, Manala and Litho, which fell under the jurisdiction of Bophuthatswana, and Pungutsa, which fell under Lebowa. The four areas were excised from the two homelands and combined into the Mnyamana regional authority, the first step in the formation of a future KwaNdebele.

On 21 April 1972 the Nationalist Government announced to the Ndebele leadership the formation of a separate homeland for the South Ndebele, despite their wishes that the two Ndebele groups be included into one governmental authority. The decision to exclude the North Ndebele was based upon advice given by government anthropologists who persisted in their opinion that this group had been well integrated into the North Sotho and Tswana societies about them and thus could not be effectively separated from their social, cultural and political contexts. The South Ndebele, on the other hand, were held to have maintained their Nguni cultural roots to a greater degree and thus to warrant separate homeland status.

It is ironic that the contradictions inherent in an ethnocentric mindset should have been so conclusively exposed by a group who supposedly supported this policy.

Despite repeated representations from North Ndebele leaders that they wished to secede from their respective Tswana and Pedi homelands, the Pretoria government remained steadfast in its decision to exclude the North Ndebele from KwaNdebele. In February 1973 they announced that henceforth, it would only deal with officially accredited chiefs on this issue, and that North Ndebele should enter into separate negotiations with the relevant

Bophuthatswana and Lebowa authorities on the issue of secession from their respective administrations.

At this point the TNNO appears to have collapsed, and was replaced soon thereafter by the Northern amaNdebele National Organisation, whose aims were specifically the inclusion of the North Ndebele into KwaNdebele. These moves did not go unnoticed by the Homeland administrations of Bophuthatswana and Lebowa, both of whom began to mobilise their considerable resources of wealth and patronage in order to minimise the North Ndebele secessionist movement.

Key figures in this movement were Chief Shikoane Kekana II of Zebediela and the Rev Molomo, chair of NANO who, prior to 1973, had already been urging North Ndebele chiefs to secede from their respective homelands. Both men now began to organise their followers, through a vigorous campaign conducted both in the press and through the medium of personal mail. On 24 March 1978 Chief Kekana issued a press statement, claiming that the Ndebele "were tired of being the children of other ethnic groups by being distributed among the different homelands", and that "if the central government was prepared to go ahead with its policy of ethnic grouping, then it must be prepared to unscramble the egg" and allow each group its rights "wherever they were."

Molomo echoed the Chief's call and wrote letters to different Northern Ndebele chiefs urging them not to allow their subjects to vote in the coming Lebowa elections on the grounds that the homeland was foreign to them. Lebowa, he argued, had been established for the baPedi, and already the Northern Ndebele had been made to feel excluded. In a memorandum to Pretoria, he pointed out that only meetings related to tribal matters could be held, that Northern Ndebele teachers were prohibited from teaching the history of their people and that Northern Ndebele leaders had been incarcerated on flimsy pretexts. As history has shown, these protests fell upon deaf ears.

In 1977 the problems suffered by both Ndebele groups were compounded by the granting of "independence" to the territory of Bophuthatswana, under the leadership of Lucas Mangope. This process had begun some time earlier, in the late 1960s, when Tswana vigilantes began a programme of ethnic cleansing in Garankuwa, a black dormitory suburb of Pretoria. They began by ordering Ndebele residents to leave the township, but soon extended this to include all non-Tswana families.

In time this spread to other areas, and by the time Bophuthatswana was established in 1977, non-Tswana residents were being denied identification documents, trading licenses, access to housing, social benefits and mother-language education. This persecution was especially severe against Ndebele citizens who, unlike members of other ethnic groups, did not have the benefit of a "homeland" they could move to under the provisions of Pretoria apartheid planning. Understandably Tswana chauvinism, layered over the existing system of white bigotry and Apartheid racism, led many Ndebele, Northern and Southern, to organise themselves along ethnic lines.

This process of ethnic separation needs to be understood in the larger context of Apartheid planning which initially only provided for the racial segregation of the country's four main groups, so-called European, African, Indian and Coloured. One of Apartheid's main concerns was inter-racial miscegenation, most specifically between whites and any of the three other groups, and although the Immorality laws prohibited inter-racial mixing between all four groups, the only times when these were applied was when one of the parties was white.

Ethnic separation, on the other hand, extended the scope of such chauvinism to inter-black relationships, and allowed each group to initiate its own programmes of ethnic cleansing. Needless to say, parallel developments were also taking place in the Transkei, and were soon to spread to Venda and Ciskei upon their own granting of "independence" and Lebowa and Gazankulu when they were granted "self-determination". It is not difficult to see therefore, how, by 1990, when the Nationalist government and the ANC began a process of rapprochement and pacification, the country had reached the brink of a racial and ethnic holocaust.

The Pretoria Government was not unaware of such developments, and in 1976 its representatives in the township of Ga-Rankuwa were advising non-Tswana residents to exchange their houses for dwellings elsewhere before they began to feel the full consequences of Tswana ethnic discrimination, most particularly in the field of education. Mangope reinforced this by closing down Ndebele-medium schools and by ordering his police to raid the homes of political opponents.

The neighboring "homeland" of Lebowa had been granted "self-determination" in 1969, and after its first elections in 1972, its government was led by Chief Minister Cedric N Phatudi. Although Lebowa shared in the same broad ideals of ethnic separation as the Tswana state, Phatudi was much more tactful in his dealings with Ndebele groups within his jurisdiction and, for a time, many Ndebele saw secession from Bophuthatswana and a union with Lebowa as a solution to their political aspirations. However, schisms within the secessionist movement and Phatudi's extension of political patronage to Ndebele chiefs willing to abide by his policies ensured that NANO remained a spent force in Lebowa. However, when these failed, Phatudi was not above using his police against political opponents, and in 1978 Molomo was arrested and savagely beaten by the Lebowa police. However, since they could lay no charges, he was eventually released.

Chief Shikoane, on the other hand, was charged with "incitement" after he had urged his followers to boycott the Lebowa elections of 1978. Although found guilty and sentenced to a fine, Chief Shikoane continued with his campaign until the Lebowa government was able to prove a case of financial mismanagement against him. He was then deposed and replaced by one of his uncles, Mr F Mathibela Kekana, who was much more amenable to Phatudi's policies. Having lost all credibility, Shikoane retired to KwaNdebele where he died in 1981.

Despite these setbacks NANO continued with its campaign for Ndebele secession. In 1978, six South Ndebele MPs in the Lebowa government began a boycott of the Legislative Assembly, thus making common cause with the North Ndebele who had been denied access by Pretoria to a unified KwaNdebele nationhood. Although the North Ndebele were now organised under NANO, the two groups continued their dialogue and their representatives attended each other's meetings and cultural functions.

However, apart from police repression and political intimidation, it was clear that the single most powerful factor standing in the way of political unification between the two groups was their physical relocation to KwaNdebele and consequent loss of ancestral lands. As a result, when KwaNdebele achieved political separation in 1981, there was no mass exodus of North Ndebele into the new "homeland."

In 1978 a number of regional authorities were constituted into the KwaNdebele Territorial Authority, and the following year it was granted legislative assembly status, the penultimate step in Pretoria's road to "independence". By 1984 it was the home to 261,875 persons of whom 5% originated from Lebowa, 29% from Bophuthatswana and 55% had been removed from white farming areas. Despite this, the tribal elites which had motivated for the establishment of a KwaNdebele state, continued to mobilise for unity between North and South Ndebele groups. Needless to say, these were ignored by Pretoria.

The critical point in the relationship between the Ndebele and their Tswana and Pedi neighbours appears to have been reached in 1982 when a move was made by Pretoria to incorporate the district of Moutse into KwaNdebele. Moutse was predominantly inhabited by the Rathoke-Ndebele, a Sotho-speaking group which had separated from the Kekana-Ndebele in the late nineteenth century. During January 1982 its councillors had met with Pretoria officials who had reported to their minister, Piet Koornhof, that the Rathoke were eager for incorporation into KwaNdebele.

This eventually took place in August 1985, but only after a conflict had taken place between North Ndebele traditionalists, favouring incorporation into a larger Ndebele polity, and urban-based Ndebele, who opposed the wider concepts of Apartheid "homeland" independence.

In order to assert their authority over the district of Moutse, the political leadership of KwaNdebele had formed the Mbokodo, a vigilante group dedicated to removing opposition within the Ndebele state. On 1 January 1986 Mbokodo invaded the Moutse area, imposing upon its residents a reign of terror which has been equated to the actions of Inkatha in Kwazulu

Natal during the 1980s and early 1990s. The people of Moutse responded by organising mass resistance against this intimidation, leading to a series of campaigns of civil disobedience and unrest. Faced with developments in Moutse, NANO began to reconsider its stance towards incorporation into KwaNdebele, and many North Ndebele instead began to identify with the movement against Bantustan government and for a unitary South Africa.

Although plans for KwaNdebele "independence" had reached an advanced stage of definition by 1986 to the point that even its stamps had been designed and were about to be printed, the continuing waves of civil unrest within Moutse eventually spread to encompass KwaNdebele as well, and in 1987 Pretoria was forced to announce that these had been shelved indefinitely. By 1990 these had been overtaken by the CODESA negotiations, and KwaNdebele had become a footnote in South Africa's unhappy chapter of Apartheid government.

Social and economic changes at kwaMsiza

The location of KwaMsiza near Pretoria has made it possible to document their transformation from a land-based agricultural peasantry to an urban and industrialized proletariat. Prior to their move in 1953, their prevalent economic activity was one of mixed farming and cattle grazing. Small amounts of cash were earned by the men working as farm labourers, although they were generally expected to provide their time for free to the owners of Hartbeesfontein in exchange for the land they occupied and farmed on their own behalf. After their move to KwaMsiza, however, they began to rely increasingly upon the income earned by their men, working as migrant labourers in the nearby towns and on the Witwatersrand gold mines.

Some of the women also entered the service of white families as domestic workers, although these jobs were generally poorly paid. As a result, from the 1950s through to the 1970s, the demographic composition of the village began to be transformed dramatically, with an increasing bias towards women and children below the age of 16. Although the men did return home, on a regular basis, this was only for a month of every year on their annual leave.

The adverse effects that the migrant labour system of Apartheid brought about upon the personal lives of rural families have been widely documented and need not be detailed here. In the case of KwaMsiza one of its more noticeable effects was an increasing focus upon the role of women in their society, and the leadership roles they began to play in their social structures. As the focus of agricultural labour fell increasingly upon the shoulders of women, so then their families became increasingly reliant upon them, where mothers not only exercised greater controls over food production and their homesteads, but over other resources as well.

This was in sharp contrast with the historical values of Ndebele society, where the men are the heads of the family (patrilocal), and give their names to the family line (patrilineal). Thus, the migrant labour system also placed traditional family and social values under severe stress. The result was that the women continued to pay lip service to the principles of patrifocality but effectively established matrilocal controls over resources and began to develop a visual system of symbology, centered on their use of beadwork and painted wall motifs, to signify a growing matrilinearity. It does not appear that this growing polychromatic decorative movement was intended to supplant the historical symbols of their men, but merely to give Ndebele society an added social dimension parallel to its traditional established order.

In 1976 a country-wide drought followed by riots and an economic downturn caused widespread unemployment, and the men of KwaMsiza began to return home, resulting in many of the older patrifocal patterns of family life being re-established. This was assisted from 1979 onwards, when the availability of employment in the nearby industrial suburb of Rosslyn, made it possible for a semblance of normality to return to this community. However many of the cultural patterns, social and material, initiated by the women in the post-1953 era have been maintained, whilst some older symbols of patrifocality have suffered a concomitant reduction in status.

This has been most noticeable in the marked shift in the location of the cattle byre. Originally this was a central circular space which acted as the focus of the community, and provided the men with an area to gather, drink beer and discuss the affairs of the village. Many of the community's rituals were centered about the byre, and the space in the upper part of the circle given over to the cattle also acted as a burial ground for their deceased. The link between the byre and their ancestors is therefore inescapable.

The Msiza and Bophuthatswana

The final blow to the Msiza's depleted finances came on 6 December 1977 when the South African government proclaimed the "independent" state of Bophuthatswana, and the district of Odi was incorporated into one of its six scattered fragments. The idea of creating a number of rurally-based independent Homeland states based upon the white government's perception of "ethnic" divisions in South Africa's black population was intended to be the culmination of Apartheid's policy of social engineering.

It was based upon Verwoerd's vision of a balkanized South African society where each of the country's nine "tribal" groupings was to be allocated its own homeland area to govern independently. The inadequacies and contradictions of such a policy were self-evident to all but their originators, and it never achieved much meaningful recognition either in South Africa or overseas. Nonetheless the existence of a Tswana ethnically-based state was to create untold hardships for the Msiza for the next sixteen years.

This hardship took many forms. The first came almost immediately when the South African Tourist Board cut off its subsidy of paint and building materials to the village, and took KwaMsiza off its tourist itineraries, claiming that tourism to the area was now a matter for the Bophuthatswana government to manage. The next arose when the Bophuthatswana government refused to allow its Ndebele subjects the right to educate their children in their mother tongue, siNdebele, a Nguni dialect, claiming that all education in the Tswana state must be conducted in seTswana. Then Bophuthatswana demanded that all its Ndebele subjects swear loyalty to the Tswana state, as a precondition to being given state or state-subsidised jobs, and being issued with travel documents.

As, for the purposes of Apartheid policy, South Africa was now a "foreign state", all Ndebele were now disenfranchised, legally prevented from traveling in their own country, and rendered stateless. Driven to the point of exasperation, a number of Ndebele leaders visited Pretoria in about 1981 and requested permission to establish their own independent state of KwaNdebele in the Dennylton-Groblersdal region.

Delighted Apartheid bureaucrats saw this as visible justification of their "ethnic" policies and quickly made arrangements to add a tenth puppet state to the nine already in operation. Fortunately a popular uprising in 1986 brought these plans to an end, and the Ndebele had to wait until 1994 to have their civic rights restored fully to them. One of the results of this struggle, however, was that the village of KwaMsiza began to run out of residential land, and not wishing to impinge upon their already meagre agricultural resources, the Msiza opened negotiations for a fresh allocation of state land from Bophuthatswana. Although a stretch of open common was available alongside their village, not unexpectedly these requests were denied.

One positive development during this time was the establishment during the 1980s of the new industrial suburb of Rosslyn immediately north of Pretoria, some 20km from KwaMsiza. This increased the level of employment in the village and allowed its men to return to their homes each day, thus reasserting the structure of the nuclear family. Despite this, the historical role of tourism in supplementing the economic base of the village appeared to be beyond repair.

To make matters worse the village's water delivery system was driven by an ageing single-stroke diesel-powered water pump which, at best, could only deliver 5 litres per minute through a single water tap. By 1986 it had begun to break down to the point that, during the nation-wide drought, it could take up to 4 hours to fill a 25 litre container. As a result the community had begun to lose some of its younger families.

It was found that, as their elderly parents had begun to pass away, so then the children's links to the settlement had grown more tenuous. At the same time the prospects of better education and a higher quality of life in the city had also begun to override traditional family loyalties. At its height in 1980 KwaMsiza had been the home to some 49 families, but by 1994 this number had dropped by 20% and the village had begun to take on a run-down appearance. Few wall paintings were being maintained, and gaps had begun to appear in its architectural fabric as the homes of deceased family members were abandoned to the elements.

KwaMsiza in the post-apartheid era

KwaMsiza appears to have reached a turning point in 1993 when a local NGO, funded by a grant from the Canadian Government, put in place a new water reticulation scheme which upgraded the village's water delivery to 21 litres per minute and gave every two households access to a shared water tap. More recently, in 2001, plans have been unveiled for the opening in the village of a tourist center and a marketing facility, which will give its residents greater access to the national tourist market.

Chapter Four
Ndebele architecture and settlement patterns

Ndebele architecture and settlement patterns

Glossary of Ndebele building terms
APOKORWAN - Eaves overhang

AMAKAPA - Roof

AMAKAPA IBALELO - Timber roof rafter

AMAOBA - Enclosed room located in the verandah

AMATHURI - Verandah

IBADI - Door

IBALELO - Used to signify a roof timber spanning from post to post, or from roof beam to roof beam, and could mean either a batten, or a ring beam

IBODA - The drum wall of a cone on cylinder dwelling

- IFESDIRI - A window. The term has probably been derived from the Dutch venster, also meaning a window opening

- IKHUPHU - The clay plaster on a wall

- IMBHEJUNI - Decorative mouldings or sculptures on a wall

- INDLU - Can be used to mean a home, or just an indoor residential space, or room

- INGODO - Timber posts supporting the outside perimeter of a verandah

- INTUTHI - The tie-beam or tie-piece at the indoor apex of a roof. This is usually used to hold in place a central post supporting the roof apex during construction. After thatching has been completed, this is removed, leaving the tie-piece behind

- ISANGO - Can be used to denote either the doorway, or the threshold to the doorway
- ISIDLOGORWANA - The capping at the roof apex
- ISITUPE - External perimeter seat surrounding the external perimeter of a dwelling
- ITHURI - The low wall enclosing a verandah room
- IZIKO - The hearth
- NGENDLINI - The raised floor inside the dwelling

- UBULONGO - The clay and cow dung finish to a floor

- UMSAMO - An internal seat located at the rear of a dwelling, on axis with the doorway and the hearth

Dwelling forms

Current archaeological evidence indicates that, up to the late 1800, South Ndebele homes and settlement patterns were very similar in both form and construction to those found in their old homeland in northern KwaZulu. Their dwellings were probably built in the form of a thatched dome, and were set in a circle about a central cattle byre.

During the 1860s they came under increasing pressure from immigrant white groups who were attempting to force them off their ancestral lands. As a result they entered into an alliance with their more powerful neighbours, the Pedi, whose territories were likewise threatened. It is probable that at this point their architecture began to adopt increasingly the forms, textures, construction, and even the decorations of the Pedi. It may be that this was an inevitable result of social interaction between the two groups, but it is also possible that this was a conscious decision taken by the Ndebele for political reasons, as the Pedi were never defeated by the Dutch and had managed to steadfastly retain control of their lands in the face of a strong white settler presence.

After the 1880s the Ndebele began to build their dwellings in the form of a central drum, some six to eight metres in diameter, surmounted by a conical thatched roof. The front of the unit was faced by a narrow enclosed verandah about 150cm wide, which ran from about 4 o'clock to 8 o'clock on the floor plan. This was used as a storage area as well as a sleeping space for young children. The central circular space was used by the parents as a sleeping area, with the left-hand side being deemed the side of the woman, the right the side of the man.

Thus the left was called the side of life, where a woman would give birth, while the right was the side of death, where a body might be laid out prior to burial. At the back of the dwelling, on axis with the doorway, was the umsamo, a residual feature from the Ndebele's ancestral architecture. Among the Nguni of KwaZulu the umsamo consists of a semi-circular raised shelf located at the back of the dwelling. It functions primarily as a storage space for food and household utensils, but is also reputed to be the home of the family's ancestral spirits, or shades, and thus also serves a spiritual space for the men.

It appears that during the transition from the Nguni thatched dome to a Pedi cone-on-cylinder structure, the original function of the umsamo was lost, and although its name remains, it no longer functions as a household storage space. Instead it has now been converted by the Ndebele into a formal seat built in clay against the back wall. This change in function was further emphasized by a move of the hearth off its central position and to the rear of the dwelling, closer to the umsamo.

The dwelling was accessed through a walled front courtyard, which was used by the women of the household for a variety of social and household functions. Additional units, usually a kitchen and sleeping quarters for the children were located off a rear courtyard, which was accessed via a side passage.

The practice of decorating the walls of the Ndebele home probably originated from their Pedi neighbours whose monochromatic "union jack" pattern survives among the Ndebele to the present day.

Settlement patterns

The similarities existing between the domestic architecture of the Ndebele and that of the Pedi was also extended to their settlement forms. Historically the larger Ndebele settlement was built in the shape of an open fan, with a large circular space containing the cattle byre and the gathering place for the men being located at its center. The dwelling of the first wife of the senior man was located at the head of the settlement, on axis with the main entry to the central space. Other wives of the senior man were then allocated homes on either side of the first wife, on a left-and-right basis in alternating order of status.

The homes of his brothers, or other members of his retinue, were located alternatively to the left and right of his abode, in descending order of status. Where such men also had polygamous families, their own homes were also structured according to an internal left-and-right ordering. Married male children were usually allocated dwellings behind that of their mother, and they too followed a left-and-right ordering. However, by the third generation the demand for space rendered all such pretense for hierarchy nonsensical, and the settlement was either reformed, or it divided into two separate homesteads.

By the 1940s most Ndebele settlements had changed to a linear pattern. The homes of individual family members were still laid out according to their status in a left-and-right hierarchy, but the homestead now followed the land's lines of contour, an arrangement which made better use of their farming resources. The cattle byre, although still central, was now in a square shape, and was located opposite the home of the senior member of the family. This was the pattern followed by the Msiza at their home at Hartbeesfontein, which they then reproduced when they were relocated to KwaMsiza in 1953.

In time, however, the village began to develop along new and innovative lines, quite different from those followed by the Ndebele previously. The original settlement at KwaMsiza was laid out in a shallow V-shape, with the Msiza family setting out their homes along one arm, while the Bhuda and Skosana took up residence along the opposite arm. The settlement was north facing and located out roughly parallel to the main road some 200m to their north.

Their agricultural lands were situated behind their homes, downhill and towards the river. Consequently, when their male children began to marry, they could not be settled on land behind their mothers, as this was too valuable a resource to be used as residential space, but rather were given land north of the original settlement, opposite their parental homes. The land between the two sides was left empty, to be used in common. As a result, the two parts of the settlement come together to enclose a village common, giving rise to a space unique in Ndebele architecture.

Although the developments recorded in Ndebele architecture over the past century are in themselves exciting, they also need to be read in the wider context of socio-economic and political changes in the southern African region. They took place at a time when this group saw the loss of its military and political power; the dispossession and occupation of their lands; the placing of whole families into indentured employment on white-owned farms; and the channeling of their men-folk in to a migrant labour system which separated them from their families for years at a time.

The latter began to establish some of the preconditions for the undermining of Ndebele patrifocal patterns and their replacement with some elements of matrifocality. Ndebele women thus responded to these forces threatening the survival of their families and of their larger Ndebele polity. They established firm controls over local resources and family structures, and reinforced the identity of their group by devision and promulgating a language of decoration which has since become identified as being uniquely Ndebele.

Their architecture therefore stands as a denial of white racist and colonial preconceptions which saw Ndebele society as being governed by "indolent, lustful and sexist polygamous males" to be broken up and channeled into a labour market for their purported "common good"; it stands as a tribute to the ability of Ndebele men and women to come together and combat the combined threats of colonialism, capitalism and apartheid; and it stands as a symbol of their spirit and their political power, their ability to take the initiative and, in a pacifist manner, reconstitute Ndebele group identify.

Chapter Five
The role of gender in Ndebele architecture
Gender roles in Ndebele home-making

From the 1940s onwards the settlement at Hartbeesfontein began to be visited increasingly by researchers, including Barrie Biermann, Constance Stuart-Larrabee, Dick Findlay, Alexis Preller and Prof AL Meiring who, together with architectural students from the University of Pretoria, conducted a survey of its architecture. Their subsequent home at KwaMsiza proved to be similarly popular among academics. Thus, barring a brief hiatus during the 1920s and 1930s, some aspects of their built environment, most particularly their wall decorations, have been particularly well documented.

Consequently the village of KwaMsiza is an important example of Ndebele architecture, for it not only does provides a strong and unbroken link to the built environment of the Ndebele during the nineteenth century, but also because it has retained its homogenous social make-up, being composed entirely of Ndzundza Ndebele families originating from the farm Hartbeesfontein.

The creation of a built environment in southern Africa's rural areas is not merely the provision of shelter: it represents an opportunity for the community to collaborate on a project, turning what is outwardly a social occasion into a display of solidarity between the larger group and the individual family unit. This process not only lays stress upon role-playing and the individual's perceived status in society, but it is used to reinforce a sense of self-identity through participation in group activities. Thus all members of the community are considered to have a role to play in the creation of an architecture. This is often predetermined by historical conditions which allocate tasks to various gender and age groups.

In a general sense, many of the heavier tasks such as the erection of walls, the construction of a timber roof frame and the creation of a grass thatch cover are considered by the Ndebele to be the work of men. Women will assist with some of this labour, such as the mixing of clay mortar, the preparation of thatch bundles and the manufacture of sun-dried bricks. Children will often assist their mothers in such work, as well as the manufacture of grass ropes and the gathering of materials like cow dung.

The plastering of walls, the creation of homestead floor areas and any subsequent light maintenance of the structure however falls directly upon the women as the controllers of household space. This includes any subsequent application of decorative motifs to the walls. The men, on the other hand, will build and maintain those areas connected with cattle folds and male gatherings, these being considered to be "men's" spaces.

In more recent times, however, the absence of men from rural communities has forced the women into the position of having to fulfill many of the building tasks historically associated with men. This, effectively, has removed the latter from the processes of the built environment, thus reinforcing the role of women as controllers of "place" as well as "resources."

Gender spaces in Ndebele homestead planning

Historically the control of Ndebele domestic space has been subject to a number of checks and balances which regulated not only relations between the genders, but also their respective access to food resources. Although many of the resultant distributions may, over the years, have been awarded metaphorical and cosmological significances, their origins may be seen to lie in a pragmatic recognition that fundamental differences exist between the life of man and that of woman.

As a result the Ndebele concept of space control is subject to a number of seemingly conflicting interpretations. For example, the titular leadership of the homestead, whether this be monogamous or polygamous, may be seen to fall upon the husband and father, and it is generally he who represents the interests of his family in any community disputation. On the other hand, the control of the physical domestic living space falls upon the wife. This concept is of particular importance in cases of polygamous marriages where the husband is expected to rotate his residence between those of individual wives.

The definition of domestic space includes the cooking area thereby also giving woman control of food resources. Any potential conflict on this issue, however, is offset by locating surplus grain in the cattle byre or the area of men's gatherings, ostensibly to be kept in reserve for emergencies, but in reality to give men access to food resources in their own right.

The spaces internal to the homestead may also be seen to be subject to the same definition of gender values. The courtyards as well as those spaces given over to children's residences and cooking functions, are considered to be the specific concern of the wife and mother. The internal living space of the parents, on the other hand, is divided equally into an area for the woman and one for the man.

This division, being the subject of "left hand" and "right hand" considerations, may be perceived to be the result of larger cosmological concepts affecting the settlement as a whole. On the other hand the creation of such a strictly-defined area for the man inside what is essentially a woman's enclave, may also be seen to be part of the same reciprocity as that governing the symbolic control of community food resources.

The channeling of the men into the migrant labour system has had important repercussions upon Ndebele homestead architecture as well as many of their social patterns. There has been, for example, a reduction of emphasis upon those areas historically considered to be the preserve of men.

The Skosana and Bhuda cattle byres at KwaMsiza all but disappeared during the 1960s, and today only the Msiza one survives, albeit in a smaller format. Even so, it now acts as a gathering space for the men of all three families, although it is possible that rationalisation may have taken place for symbolic and political as well as practical reasons. Also to be considered is the fact that today cattle play a negligible role in the life of the community whose economy has changed almost entirely to a cash base.

It is also true that grain surpluses are no longer stored, symbolically or otherwise, in the men's gathering place. Instead these are now lodged in the cooking area of the woman concerned. This may now be done for reasons of practicality, or to reinforce the growing power of women in the group, or perhaps because the community functions that this act of communality once represented, are no longer relevant.

The reduction in the size and importance of the men's areas has not been met by a concomitant expansion of women's household space. Instead their emphasis has been a visual one, relying upon the use of complex, polychromatic graphic elements painted upon the perimeter walls of the homestead as well as those of individual dwellings.

Gender elements of Ndebele settlement

A metaphor which has been used by some Ndebele to describe their built habitat likens the spaces of the homestead to the body of a woman. In their terms the front courtyard, generally an area of "clean" activities, is likened to the mapoto or beaded apron worn by married women as part of their wedding finery; the parents' dwelling is the womb, for it is here the mother resides and hence it is the origin of the family's fertility, its children and hence its wealth. The rear quarters which house the cooking areas as well as the children are the breasts whence all nourishment originates. This symbolism is reinforced during the wedding celebrations when the men dance through the front courtyard of the bride's family homestead, thereby ritually defiling it to the accompaniment of ribald jokes from their womenfolk.

The role of decoration in Ndebele society

The beginnings of Ndebele painted wall traditions do not appear to predate the land war of 1882-3. Up to that time their architecture made extensive use of grass and reed - materials which preclude painted decoration. The origins of their wall art appear to lie with the Pedi, a neighbouring group whose architecture and decorative motifs they adopted after 1883, both of which they employ to the present day. These consist of a simple set of chevron or "Union

Jack" patterns rendered in white or black upon a plain grey background. Although Ndebele polychromatic wall art today bears scant resemblance to Pedi patterns, its roots ought to be seen to rest in the practice of rendering walls for ritual and social purposes, rather than in their actual style of decoration.

Since the late 1940s Ndebele painted wall tradition has focused increasingly upon a stylisation and rendering of the patterns and images of nearby Victorian small town architecture as well as the graphic elements of an urban consumer and industrial society further afield. The result has been the development of a complex code of images based upon colour and form which have been used to convey messages about the fertility, political rights, territorial boundaries, family lineage and regional identity of their originators. All of these elements must be seen to play a strong role in the large pattern of Ndebele gender politics.

Normally the walls outlining the perimeter of an Ndebele homestead will not be built, and hence decorated, until approximately two years after the birth of a woman's first child. Thus wall decoration is symbolic of women's fertility and serves to indicate her status in the community as a mother, head of homestead and responsible adult.

By giving birth to a child a woman also gains for her husband full participation in the community's council of men as a family head. Her work therefore is symbolic of how her fertility has given her family a voice in the public affairs of the group.

The application of wall decoration is usually also indicative of times of transition in the life of a woman, such as the marriage of a daughter, or the period when her son attends initiation school.

Wall decoration plays a strong symbolic role in the creation of living areas among those southern African groups who define their exterior living spaces. The act of painting or smearing a wall has direct links to a cosmological belief which perceives women to be inherently "hot" and men inherently "cool". Homestead boundaries are seen to be similarly "hot", most particularly where two women share the same division wall; these then need to be "cooled" by a process of wall smearing and decoration which, presumably, might also imply a degree of cooperation between the two parties concerned. Thus wall decoration not only serves to create statements of territorial control but, by implication, suggests that women are more than just passive partners to their menfolk in the control of rural household space and food resources.

A measure of heraldry is also implied in the designs of rural wall art. The act of painting is conducted either by the mother, or by her teenage daughters under her direct guidance. The complex patterns are thus part of the young girl's training and are reinforced when, upon marriage, she is presented by her mother with a partly-finished beaded apron, the mapoto, bearing the essential elements of this design. The daughter is then expected to complete the apron after her marriage. Although in theory the young bride may choose to decorate her walls in whatever pattern she wishes, in reality, her first design seldom strays far from that which she learnt at home as a child and which she carried away with her in a shorthand form as part of her wedding dowry.

A clue as to the more fundamental reasons underlying the development of a wall decorating tradition among the Ndebele may be found in the struggle for land which has taken place in southern Africa over the past two centuries, between indigenous black and immigrant white groups. The ZAR-Ndzundza war of 1883 must therefore be seen in the context of the fact that, since 1811, the South African region has seen 24 major conflicts and over two score smaller localized conflagrations. This means that, on average, one major rebellion, war or uprising has taken place here every third year for the past 179 years.

The reasons recorded for these conflicts are many and varied. The majority however may be seen to have been the result of competition for land between white and black rural groups. The single most important source of friction between these two therefore must lie in the control, or lack of, that each exercises over agricultural land.

It may be argued that the aesthetics of wall decoration have played an important role in reinforcing (or perhaps even creating) a unique regional identity for the Ndebele whose land is currently in the holding of descendants of the very farmers who defeated them over a century ago.

The chronology of Ndebele wall art therefore places it firmly into a time when formal resistance to white political dominance was at a low; when the effects of the rural land acts were beginning to become evident; when rural poverty was beginning to spread; when rural women began to find their men being channeled in increasing numbers into a system of migrant labour; when whites across the virtual spectrum of political opinion saw blacks as being voteless, dispossessed and landless in perpetuity; and at a time when formal black resistance was limited to an ANC which had but recently adopted a more confrontational stance. It was during this time that Ndebele women took up the cudgels of their people's struggle and began to decorate their homestead walls, making statements about their social conditions and creating images of regional and political identity.

It is also significant to note that the Ndebele use of wall decorations is not limited to the outward facades of their perimeter wall and their dwellings but, in most cases, have also been located inside and at the back of the parent's unit, above the umsamo. Historically in Nguni society, the umsamo has been regarded as a male area and the residence of the family's "shades" or ancestral spirits. In current Ndebele society however, it has been converted into a seat and the wall behind it is decorated with the major components of the wife's heraldic patterns. The internal hearth, another ancient symbol of woman, has been moved away from its old location at the centre of the dwelling, and has been relocated closer to the umsamo.

Social and Cultural Life

Internal political and social structures

Ndebele authority structures were similar to those of their Zulu cousins. The authority over a tribe was vested in the tribal head (ikozi), assisted by an inner or family council(amaphakathi). Wards (izilindi) were administered by ward heads and the family groups within the wards were governed by the heads of the families. The residential unit of each family was called an umuzi The umuzi usually consisted of a family head (umnumzana) with his wife and unmarried children. If he had more than one wife, the umuzi was divided into two halves, a right and a left half, to accommodate the different wives. An umuzi sometimes grew into a more complex dwelling unit when the head's married sons and younger brothers joined the household. Every tribe consisted of a number of patrilineal clans or izibongo. This meant that every clan consisted of a group of individuals who shared the same ancestor in the paternal line.

Division of Labor

In a pastoral society such as that of the Ndebele, men attended to animal husbandry and women to horticultural and agricultural activities except when new fields (amasimu) are cleared with the help of men who join in a communal working party called an ijima. Even male social age status is defined in terms of husbandry activities: a boy who herds goats (umsana wembuzana), a boy who herds calves (umsana wamakhonyana), and so forth. Men are responsible for the construction and thatching of houses, women for plastering and painting of walls. Teenage girls are trained by their mothers in the art of smearing and painting. Even today girls from an early age (approximately 5 or 6) assist their mothers in the fetching of water and wood, making fire, and cooking. Female responsibilities have arduously increased in recent years with the increase in permanent and temporary male and female labor migrants to urban areas. It is calculated that some 80 percent of rural KwaNdebele residents are labor migrants.

Personal adornment

Ndebele women traditionally adorned themselves with a variety of ornaments, each symbolising her status in society. After marriage, dresses became increasingly elaborate and spectacular. In earlier times, the Ndebele wife would wear copper and brass rings around her arms, legs and neck, symbolising her bond and faithfulness to her husband, once her home was built. She would only remove the rings after his death.

The rings (called idzila) were believed to have strong ritual powers. Husbands used to provide their wives with rings; the richer the husband, the more rings the wife would wear. Today, it is no longer common practice to wear these rings permanently. In addition to the rings, married women also wore neck hoops made of grass (called isigolwani) twisted into a coil and covered in beads, particularly for ceremonial occasions.

Isigolwani are sometimes worn as neckpieces and as leg and arm bands by newly wed women whose husbands have not yet provided them with a home, or by girls of marriageable age after the completion of their initiation ceremony. Married women also wore a five-fingered apron (called an ijogolo) to mark the culmination of the marriage, which only takes place after the birth of the first child.

The marriage blanket (nguba) worn by married women was decorated with beadwork to record significant events throughout the woman's lifetime. For example, long beaded strips signified that the woman's son was undergoing the initiation ceremony and indicated that the woman had now attained a higher status in Ndebele society. It symbolised joy because her son had achieved manhood as well as the sorrow at losing him to the adult world.

A married woman always wore some form of head covering as a sign of respect for her husband. These ranged from a simple beaded headband or a knitted cap to elaborate beaded headdresses (amacubi). Boys usually ran around naked or wore a small front apron of goatskin. However, girls wore beaded aprons or beaded wraparound skirts from an early age. For rituals and ceremonies, Ndebele men adorned themselves with ornaments made for them by their wives.

Art and Crafts

Ndebele art has always been an important identifying characteristic of the Ndebele. Apart from its aesthetic appeal it has a cultural significance that serves to reinforce the distinctive Ndebele identity. The Ndebele's essential artistic skill has always been understood to be the ability to combine exterior sources of stimulation with traditional design concepts borrowed from their ancestors. Ndebele artists also demonstrated a fascination with the linear quality of elements in their environment and this is depicted in their artwork. Painting was done freehand, without prior layouts, although the designs were planned beforehand. The characteristic symmetry, proportion and straight edges of Ndebele decorations were done by hand without the help of rulers and squares. Ndebele women were responsible for painting the colourful and intricate patterns on the walls of their houses.

This presented the traditionally subordinate wife with an opportunity to express her individuality and sense of self-worth. Her innovativeness in the choice of colours and designs set her apart from her peer group. In some instances, the women also created sculptures to express themselves. The back and side walls of the house were often painted in earth colours and decorated with simple geometric shapes that were shaped with the fingers and outlined in black. The most innovative and complex designs were painted, in the brightest colours, on the front walls of the house.

The front wall that enclosed the courtyard in front of the house formed the gateway (izimpunjwana) and was given special care. Windows provided a focal point for mural designs and their designs were not always symmetrical. Sometimes, makebelieve windows are painted on the walls to create a focal point and also as a mechanism to relieve the geometric rigidity of the wall design. Simple borders painted in a dark colour, lined with white, accentuated less important windows in the inner courtyard and in outside walls. Contemporary Ndebele artists make use of a wider variety of colours (blues, reds, greens and yellows) than traditional artists were able to, mainly because of their commercial availability.

Traditionally, muted earth colours, made from ground ochre, and different natural-coloured clays, in white, browns, pinks and yellows, were used. Black was derived from charcoal. Today, bright colours are the order of the day. As Ndebele society became more westernised, the artists started reflecting this change of their society in their paintings. Another change is the addition of stylised representational forms to the typical tradtional abstract geometric designs. Many Ndebele artists have now also extended their artwork to the interior of houses.

Ndebele artists also produce other crafts such as sleeping mats and isingolwani. Isingolwani (colourful neck hoops) are made by winding grass into a hoop, binding it tightly with cotton and decorating it with beads. In order to preserve the grass and to enable the hoop to retain its shape and hardness, the hoop is boiled in sugar water and left in the hot sun for a few days. A further outstanding characteristic of the Ndebele is their beadwork. Beadwork is intricate and time consuming and requires a deft hand and good eyesight. This pastime has long been a social practice in which the women engaged after their chores were finished but today, many projects involve the production of these items for sale to the public.

Ndebele aesthetic expression in the form of mural art and beadwork has won international fame for that society during the latter half of the twentieth century. Mural painting (*ukugwala*) is done by women and their daughters and entails the multicolor application of acrylic paint on entire outer and inner courtyard and house walls. Earlier paints were manufactured and mixed from natural material such as clay, plant pulp, ash, and cow dung. Since the 1950s, mural patterns have shown clear urban and Western influences. Consumer goods (e.g., razor blades), urban architecture (e.g., gables, lampposts), and symbols of modern transportation (e.g., airplanes, number plates) acted as inspiration for women artists.

Beadwork (*ukupothela*) also proliferated during the 1950s; it shows similarity in color and design to murals.

Ndebele beadwork is essentially part of female ceremonial costume. Beads are sown on goat skins, canvas, and even hard board nowadays, and worn as aprons. Beaded necklaces and arm and neck rings form part of the outfit that is worn during rituals such as initiation and weddings. As Ndebele beadwork became one of the most popular curio art commodities in the period from the mid-1960s to the mid-1990s, women also beaded glass bottles, gourds, and animal horns. The recent prolific trading in Ndebele beadwork concentrates on "antique" garments as pieces of art. Some women are privately commissioned to apply their painting on canvas, shopping center walls, and even cars.

The recent discourse on Ndebele art suggests that the phenomenon should be interpreted in terms of the conscious establishment of a distinctive ethnic Ndebele niche at a time in South African history when the

Ndebele struggled to regain their land and were not regarded as a society with its own identity.

Courtship and marriage

Marriages were only concluded between members of different clans, that is between individuals who did not have the same clan name. However, a man could marry a woman from the same family as his paternal grandmother. The prospective bride was kept secluded for two weeks before the wedding in a specially made structure in her parents' house, to shield her from men's eyes.

When the bride emerged from her seclusion, she was wrapped in a blanket and covered by an umbrella that was held for her by a younger girl who also attended to her other needs. On her marriage, the bride was given a marriage blanket, which she would, in time, adorn with beadwork, either added to the blanket's outer surface or woven into the fabric. After the wedding, the couple lived in the area belonging to the husband's clan. Women retained the clan name of their fathers but children born of the marriage took their father's clan name.

Belief System

In traditional Ndebele society it was believed that illnesses were caused by an external force such as a spell or curse that was put on an individual. The power of a traditional healer was measured by his or her ability to defeat this force. Cures were either effected by medicines or by throwing bones. All traditional medicine men and women (izangoma) were mediums, able to contact ancestral spirits. Some present-day Ndebele still adhere to ancestral worship but many have subsequently become Christians and belong to the mainstream Christian churches or to one of the many local Africanised churches.

Chapter Six
Ndebele Religion and Expressive Culture
Religious Beliefs

Nineteenth-century evangelizing activities by the Berlin Mission did little to change traditional Ndebele religion, especially that of the Ndzundza. Although the Manala lived on the Wallmannsthal mission station from 1873, they were in frequent conflict with local missionaries. Recent Christian and African Christian church influences spread rapidly, however, and most Ndebele are now members of the Zion Christian Church (ZCC), one of a variety of (African) Apostolic churches, or the Catholic church. Traditional beliefs were centered on a creator god, Zimu, and ancestral spirits (*abezimu*).

Religious Practitioners.

Disgruntled ancestral spirits cause illness, misfortune, and death. Traditional practitioners (*iinyanga* and *izangoma*) act as mediators between the past and present world and are still frequently consulted. Sorcerers (abathakathi or abaloyi) are believe to use familiars like the well-known "baboon" midget (*utikoloshe*), especially in cases of jealousy toward achievers in the community in general. Both women and men become healers after a prolonged period of internship with existing practitioners.

Ceremonies.

Initiation at puberty dominates ritual life in Ndebele society. Girls' initiation (*iqhude* or *ukuthombisa*) is organized on an individual basis, within the homestead. It entails the isolation of a girl after her second or third menstruation in an existing house in the homestead, which is prepared by her mother. The weeklong period of isolation ends over the weekend, when as many as two hundred relatives, friends, and neighbors attend the coming-out ritual.

The occasion is marked by the slaughtering of cows and goats, cooking and drinking of traditional beer (*unotlhabalala*), song and dance, and the large-scale presentation of gifts (clothing and toiletries) to the initiate's mother and rather. In return, the initiate's mother presents large quantities of bread and jam to attendants. The notion of reciprocity is prominent. During the iqhude, women sing, dance, and display traditional costumes as the men remain spatially isolated from the courtyard in front of the homestead.

Male initiation (*ingoma* or *ukuwela*), which includes circumcision, *is* a collective and quadrennial ritual that lasts two months during the winter (April to June). The notion of cyclical regimentation is prominent: initiates in the postliminal stage receive a regimental name from the paramount, and it is this name with which an Ndebele man identifies himself for life. The Ndzundza-Ndebele have a system of fifteen such names that are used over a period of approximately sixty years. The cycle repeats itself in strict chronological order. The Manala-Ndebele have thirteen names.

The numerical dimension of Ndebele male initiation is unparalleled in southern Africa. During the 1985 initiation, some 10,000 young men were initiated and, during 1993, more than 12,000. The ritual is controlled, installed, officiated, and administered by the royal house. It is decentralized over a wide area within the former KwaNdebele, in rural as well as urban (township) areas. Regional headmen (see "Political

Organization") are assigned to supervise the entire ritual process over the two-month period, which involves nine sectional rituals at *emphadwini* (lodges in the field) and *emzini* (lodges at the homestead).

Medicine.

Current medical assistance includes the simultaneous use and application of traditional cures and medicines and visits to local hospitals and clinics. Children are born with or without the assistance of modern maternity care.

Death and Afterlife.

Death is attributed to both natural and supernatural causes. A period of night watch over the body precedes the funeral. Funerals reunite the homestead and family members and involve the recital of clan praises (*iibongo*) at the grave and the slaughtering of animals at the deceased's homestead afterward. Today many

Ndebele receive church burials. Widows are regarded as unclean; they may be ritually cleansed after many months or even a year. Traditionally, the deceased are buried at family grave sites, which are usually at the ruins of previous settlements and often far away from their homes. Nowadays, however, people are mostly buried at nearby cemeteries.

www.ingramcontent.com/pod-product-compliance
Lightning Source LLC
Chambersburg PA
CBHW021113080526
44587CB00010B/501